Kaaterskill
From the Catskill Mountain House
to the
Hudson River School

Mountain Top Historical Society

BLACK · DOME

BLACK DOME PRESS CORP.
RR 1, Box 422
Hensonville, NY 12439
Tel: (518) 734-6357
Fax: (518) 734-5802

First Edition 1993
Published by Black Dome Press Corp.
RR1, Box 442
Hensonville, NY 12439
Tel: (518)734-6357
Fax: (518)734-5802

Library of Congress Catalog Card Number: 93-079369

ISBN 0-9628523-8-4

All or portions of essays by Manos, Kudish, Hommel,Helmer, and West first appeared in *Catskill Center News*, the newsletter of the Catskill Center for Conservation and Development, Arkville, NY and *The Hemlock*, the newsletter of the Mountain Top Historical Society.

Proofreading by Patricia H. Davis

Printed in the USA

Dedication

Twenty years ago, a small group gathered to form what is today's Mountain Top Historical Society. The Society cannot hope to acknowledge adequately the innumerable individuals who have given unstintingly of their time over the past two decades. We do, however, wish to express very special gratitude to one of our founders, our current president, and an extraordinarily gifted woman. This volume, published in the year of our twentieth anniversary is dedicated to Justine Hommel, whose labor and dedication have been vital to our history and success.

The Mountain Top Historical Society

Contents

Introduction

The Sublime Kaaterskill

Bob Gildersleeve

A few miles west of the Hudson River, about 120 miles north of New York City and 40 miles south of Albany, a small stretch of undeveloped land has inspired people of vastly different interests in ways far beyond its limited boundaries. Here no extensive battles were fought, nor did any great turning point of our history occur. The area is easily missed by travelers on the New York State Thruway as they rush between New York City and Albany. It is even lightly dismissed by winter vacationers hurrying to the local ski slopes, passing obliviously through its main corridor. Yet to those who discover it, the Kaaterskill region is sublime. In fact, sublime is perhaps the most frequent word used by the Romantic writers of the 19th century in describing this area. But the sense of the sublime—so essential to American and European Romantics—seems lost to us as the 20th century closes. It is a great loss, but the character of this region that helped define America's sense of itself a century and a half ago remains unchanged. When we leave our cars and walk for an hour along a Kaaterskill trail, the sense of the sublime begins to return. It is easy to see how this small stretch of wilderness inspired artists and poets to exquisite expressions of their wonder.

Our intention in publishing *Kaaterskill* is to bring together in a brief guide the major themes that have made the Kaaterskill region unique.

Geologists have studied the area since the early days of the Mountain House. Before geologists had access to the Grand Canyon and at a time when our understanding of glaciers and the ice age was just developing, the Kaaterskill provided an excellent locale. Constantine Manos is professor of Geology at State University of New York at New Paltz and its Department Chair. In describing the geology of the Kaaterskill area, his article reflects the recent revolution in geologic thought, that of plate tectonics.

The diverse forest of the region attracted scientists of America and Europe as well as the Romantic artist and vacationer. Michael Kudish, assistant professor of forestry at Paul Smith's College in Paul Smiths, New York, has spent many summers in the Catskills, the vegetational history of which was the subject of his Ph. D. dissertation. His in-depth studies of the Catskill forest are a rare combination of scientific accuracy and general readability.

At the hub of this activity and the great proponent of it were the magnificent hotels. And no one, perhaps, is better equipped to write about them than Justine Hommel. Ms. Hommel is a founder of the Mountain Top Historical Society and its guiding spirit. A native resident of Haines Falls, she, unlike many of us, has not been blinded to the uniqueness of the area by her proximity to it. As librarian of the Haines Falls Library she was able to research the history of the most popular hotels and collect stories of the locality. She has contributed to the work of virtually every modern student of the area and, fortunately, to this guide as well.

Now that they are gone, the railroads that brought vacationers to the Kaaterskill have a romantic character of their own. William Helmer is author of *Rip Van Winkle Railroads*, the definitive study of the railroads of the Kaaterskill region, and was the natural person to approach for an article on that subject. To my joy, and the good fortune of all who read this, he accepted.

The best way to see the Kaaterskill region now, as it has always been, is on foot. Edward West, former Superintendent of Land Acquisition for the New York State Department of Conservation, knew this area as well as any person, having surveyed much of it for the State of New York and having explored it for the joy of doing so.

It took landscape artists and poets to tell the world of this area. Professor Alfred Marks' 1980 course on the region at the State University of New York at New Paltz inspired the booklet *Kaaterskill Profile*. Several of the works included in the present volume first appeared in that publication. The Society is indebted to the Catskill Center for Conservation and Development for its generous contribution to that publication and its support of this volume.

Alfred H. Marks has written an article on the writers of the region. His piece will introduce many of you to Bliss Carmen. Dr. Marks is Professor Emeritus of American Literature at State University of New York at New Paltz, where he served for ten years as Director of the Carl Carmer Center for Catskill Mountain and Hudson River Studies. He is now New Paltz town and village historian.

Raymond Beecher is a long-time resident of Greene County with an active interest in its history. A Coxsackie town historian, past president of the Greene County Historical Society, former curator of the Bronck Museum and, for almost three decades, its Vedder Memorial librarian, he has written extensively and also assisted others in promoting a better understanding of Greene County's historical development.

Defining the center of this area both geographically and inspirationally was the Catskill Mountain House. Roland Van Zandt was author of the definitive book on the subject, *The Catskill Mountain House*. We are fortunate to be able to include a previously unpublished article on the Mountain House in this publication.

If you have hiked the trails around North Lake and wondered about the history of the area, we hope this guide will provide some insights. If you picked up *Kaaterskill* because of an interest in the region, we hope this guide will provide incentive to explore the area first-hand.

Pioneers

"I have traveled the woods for many years," said Leather-Stocking, "...and I can say that I have met but one place that was more to my liking; and that was only to eyesight, and not for hunting or fishing."

"And where was that?" asked Edwards.

"Where! why, up on the Catskills...the place I mean is next to the river, where one of the ridges juts out a little from the rest, and where the rocks fall for the best part of a thousand feet so much up and down that a man standing on their edges is fool enough to think he can jump from top to bottom."

"What see you when you get there?" asked Edwards.

"Creation!" said Natty,..."all creation, lad."

James Fenimore Cooper

Preface

Roland Van Zandt

Historians found little to attract them to the subject of the Catskill Mountains, and the few books that appeared, such as John Burrough's *In the Catskills* (1910), T. Morris Longstreth's *The Catskills* (1918), and H. A. Haring's *Our Catskill Mountains* (1931), were essentially travel books that were practically devoid of history. It is all reminiscent of Jefferson's remark that "wars and contentions...fill the pages of history.... But more blest is that nation whose silent course of happiness furnishes nothing for history to say."

But then as I say, there was very little past in the Catskills to be vibrant about—or so I assumed until I saw those bewitching ruins. They were a manifestation of considerable power and ambition, and must have been the excrescence of some formidable movement in the larger national background. Such turned out to be the case, as I discovered during the next five years of research.

The original Catskill Mountain House (which remained embedded in all subsequent additions) was built in 1823 when Thomas Jefferson and John Adams were still alive, the American frontier lay west of the Mississippi River, and the Catskill Mountains were an empty wilderness save for a few primitive settlements. Inns and taverns, of course, abounded in the rising cities of the Atlantic seaboard, where they had been known from the time of the earliest settlements. But except for a few watering-places such as Saratoga, where people of wealth and fashion congregated during summer months to escape the pestilential diseases of the coastal regions and to enjoy what were called the "health restoring properties" of the mineral springs, hotels built solely for pleasure and entertainment—in other words, "resorts"—were nonexistent. The Mountain House was not only the first such hotel in the Catskills, but was also one of the first in America, and it was one of the nation's first <u>mountain</u> resorts as well.

From the time it opened its doors in 1824 as a sumptuous 10-room "house of entertainment" until the end of the century, when it had become a monolithic 315-room palace with miles of trails and carriage roads, two lakes, a 3,000-acre park, its own railroad and cable-cars from the Hudson River to its very doorstep, the Mountain House remained one of the most expensive, luxurious, and fashionable resorts in all North America, drawing its patronage from the elite of society on both sides of the Atlantic, its fame spread from the Court of Queen Victoria to the dynastic capitals of the Orient. The registers of the hotel read like a veritable *Who's Who* of 19th-century society: ambassadors, cabinet members, European royalty, famous writers, artists, actors, inventors, several leading generals of the Civil War, and two or three American presidents—these and hosts of others enhanced the fame of the Mountain House.

Preface

"If you want to see the sights of America," James Fenimore Cooper told his European audience in the 1850's, "go to see Niagara Falls, Lake George, and the Catskill Mountain House." As provincial as this sounds to us today, it had more than a grain of truth in the first half of the 19th century. America at that time was a regional rather than continental power, New York State had recently become the wealthiest and most populous state in the union, and the Hudson valley had become the nation's leading thoroughfare of trade and commerce. The new hotel in the Catskills stood in the center of this, the only hotel accessible for a two or three night's visit—and later on a fortnight's vacation—from the largest city in the nation.

The Mountain House was almost immediately a famous landmark of the American landscape, and the image of the white colossus with its thirteen Corinthian columns became a favorite of the reproductive arts of the 19th century. It was pictured on thousands of postcards; engraved on souvenir and memorial spoons; etched into paperweights and the handles of letter openers; and baked into Staffordshire china. It became familiar to a broad middle-class public who subscribed to such popular magazines as *Harper's* and *The Atlantic Monthly*, and a most familiar subject of those ubiquitous stereoscopic views. It was featured year after year in railroad and steamship literature; appeared in countless guide books and "annuals" and picture books of the period; was immortalized by Currier and Ives; and as one of America's finest examples of neo-classic architecture, it was engraved, aquatinted, and painted in oils by a legion of artists and illustrators, good and bad, famous and obscure, from its opening well into the present century. Perhaps only the mighty Niagara Falls or the famous battlements of West Point were more familiar to the 19th-century American. The Mountain House was, in fact, a national treasure.

The Falls of Cauterskill in Winter

Winter, hoary, stern, and strong,
Sits the mountain crags among;
On his bleak and horrid throne,
Drift on drift the snow is piled,
Into forms grotesque and wild;
Ice-ribbed precipices shed
Cold light round his grizzly head.
Clouds athwart his brows are bound,
Ever whirling round and round.

Thomas Cole

When Nature Met Art: The Hudson River School

by Raymond Beecher

With few exceptions, they came during the months of clement weather to capture in pencil, charcoal, and oil the landscape they considered to be "the heart of the Catskills." They came to that area north of Kaaterskill Clove, which encompasses North and South Mountains, and which was overshadowed by the higher, less accessible peaks. In this one small corner of the Mountain Top were to be found those aspects of American landscape which appealed so strongly to the nineteenth-century artists—a dramatic vista stretching in a wide arc including the mid-Hudson River Valley and easterly into New England, spectacularly beautiful. Here also were to be found two small wilderness-like lakes, draining for a short distance and then plunging abruptly down one of the highest waterfalls in the eastern United States, and a fantastic "man-made" edifice, the Catskill Mountain House, so dramatically situated in the midst of this scenic paradise.

And come these artists did: Thomas Cole, Jasper Cropsey, John F. Kensett, Sanford R. Gifford, Thomas Doughty, Jarvis McEntee, Asher B. Durand, and Frederic Church, all major figures in the first and second generations of the Hudson River School of Art. In addition were those from the English watercolorist tradition, two such notable individuals being William Guy Wall, responsible for *Hudson River Portfolio* (1820), and William Henry Bartlett, whose typographical views appeared in N. P. Willis's *American Scenery* (1840).

Among the earliest American landscapists to gain inspiration from the northern Catskill Mountains was Thomas Cole (1801-1848). In his comparatively short lifetime, even after sketching expeditions throughout the Northeast and his two trips to Europe, Cole never lost interest in his beloved Catskills. Cedar Grove, the Thomson-Cole residence, held the Catskill range in its sight. From the village of Catskill, Cole's numerous field trips led to the Catskills, and from these expeditions came a series of controlled landscapes utilizing Kaaterskill Falls, North Mountain, the Catskill Mountain House, South Mountain, and the two lakes. Scenes in the Catskill Valley from his brush also utilized the Catskill range for background.

While some Cole dates are conjectural, art historians credit *Lake With Dead Trees* (Allen Art Museum, Oberlin College) with being among the three oils that resulted from Cole's first upriver trip in 1825. That South Lake scene, modified by symbolic tree images, was a milestone in American art. From that same sketching effort came *Cascade in Catskill Mountains* (Wadsworth Athenaeum), as viewed from the mouth of the amphitheater. Here the depiction is enhanced with shades of light reflected in water and with clouds, dark pines, and colorful autumn foliage. Cole sold that original work to John Trumbull and

produced a copy, labeled *Kaaterskill Falls*. In 1831 Fenner
Sears & Company of London published its engraving *The
Falls of Catskill, New York* based upon this Cole oil painting
on canvas. *Falls of the Kaaterskill* (Warner Collection, Gulf
States Corporation) was painted by Cole in 1826. In it he
sought to provide the viewer with a sense of the unspoiled
wilderness, the lone Indian figure adding scale to the
natural landscape. (Matthew Baigell in his volume *Thomas
Cole* credits Haines Falls as being the locale, the confusion
being caused by a mixup of the creek names. This is
disputed by some hikers who are familiar with these
narrow cloves. Until the stairs were constructed at Haines
Falls giving ready access from the summit, few travelers
and artists undertook the hazardous climb to the base of
Haines Falls.) In the same year, Cole painted *From the Top
of Kaaterskill Falls* (Detroit Institute of Art).

The years 1827-1828 were productive ones for Cole.
This period of time brought about the completion of *Sunny
Morning on the Hudson* (Boston Museum of Fine Arts) in
which Cole utilized the forested, rounded dome, dead
tree, rock, rising mist, and distant view of the Hudson
River. Additionally, from his studio came *The Clove, Catskills*
(New Britain Museum of American Art) and *The Last of the
Mohicans* based on James Fenimore Cooper's American
pioneer novel. Almost identical canvases of this re-inter-
preted site of the Catskill Mountain House ledge are held
by the New York Historical Association and by the
Wadsworth Athenaeum.

Just how early in his painting career Cole sought to
include the newly-constructed Catskill Mountain House
in his sketches is uncertain, but certainly it was within five
years of the structure's appearance. *View of the Catskill
Mountain House, New York 1828* reveals that hostelry as
seen from the tortuous road to the Pine Orchard. It is this

21

familiar scene which was engraved for *History and Topography of the United States.* Enoch Wood, the Staffordshire potter, copied the engraving for his decorated earthenware produced primarily for the American market. This same general area of ascent to the Mountain Top, including the hotel, also appears in an undated Cole production. In this work, he made use of autumn hues and South Mountain. DeWitt Clinton Boutelle painted this two-level aspect in 1845.

In 1843, after extensive traveling, Thomas Cole again turned to the Mountain Top to depict the growing fame of the Catskill Mountain House. That landscape utilized the view from North Mountain (Stillman Collection). The following year, he created *A View of the Two Lakes and the Catskill Mountain House, Morning 1844* (Brooklyn Museum). Field sketches of this North Mountain section survive in Princeton University's art museum.

The fact that the panoramic view from North Mountain, encompassing the now-famous hotel and the two picturesque lakes, was a favorite of both Bartlett and Cole did not deter either Jasper Cropsey or Sanford Robinson Gifford from repeat performances. Bartlett may well have popularized this landscape with his 1836 work engraved for Willis's *American Scenery.*

A comparison of the four efforts is unavoidable. Both Cole and Bartlett featured the human form in a hiker's stance in the foreground. Taller trees surviving the furies of nature were Bartlett additions, while Cole utilized twisted, stunted, dead trees barely surviving in a harsh environment. In one painting. Cole makes use of storm clouds, adding dramatic effect. Jasper Cropsey, in his 1855 oil on canvas entitled *Catskill Mountain House From North Mountain* (Minneapolis Institute of Arts) provides the viewer with a sharper focus. Gone is the human figure but a dead or dying tree remains. Bartlett's deer are replaced by a few airborne birds.

Like his predecessor Thomas Cole, Sanford R. Gifford experienced the beauty and awe of superior landscapes while traveling both here and abroad. Yet for all that, like Cole, Gifford drew heavily on the Catskill Mountains for his inspiration. Roland Van Zandt, in his *The Catskill Mountain House*, summarizes succinctly Gifford's admiration:

> *How important the Catskills were to Gifford may be seen by the Metropolitan Museum of Art's "Memorial Catalogue" of his work which was printed the year after his death. More than a hundred of the paintings and sketches listed in that catalogue were done in the Catskills, and the majority were painted within a four-mile radius of the Catskill Mountain House.*

Gifford's canvas *Catskill Mountains*, produced in 1868, utilizes the North Mountain foreground, reducing the lake coverage but expanding the distant view to the southeast. The Mountain House itself is a small image on the larger scene. Earlier, in 1862, Gifford used much of the same perspective as in 1868. That canvas is displayed at the Austin Arts Center of Trinity College in Hartford, Connecticut; it measures $9^5/_{16}$ by $18^1/_2$ inches, one of Gifford's smaller renditions. All four, Bartlett, Cole, Cropsey and Gifford tended toward the autumnal months of the year for added color.

After working at Boston with Champney and others, and enhanced by field work with Benjamin Champney in the White Mountains during the summer of 1851, Benjamin Bellows Grant Stone migrated to New York City where he gained additional training with Jasper Cropsey.

Stone first appears upriver at Catskill in September 1851. His diary for that year reveals that he sketched in the Mountain House environs. The following summer, he again utilized the village of Catskill for his base of operations, frequently walking to Palenville, a distance of approximately eleven miles. Landscape drawing became Stone's primary interest for the remainder of his life.

Diary entries, sketchbooks, and large single-sheet drawings which survive in the collections at the Greene County Historical Society indicate that Stone and some of his artist friends found Kaaterskill Clove and the Mountain Top of special interest. Stone mentions some of his colleagues: Edward C. Post, who had been renting Cole's old studio; Casilear; Volmere; Johnson; Arnot; and Lewis.

Several lithographic prints were produced from Stone's drawings. Of particular interest for this article is *Catskill Mountain House* produced by J. H. Bufford of Boston in 1860. In later years, a number of Stone's sketches provided an artistic touch to DeLisser's *Picturesque Catskills*. The distinctive identification may be observed as an "S" with the "T" superimposed. Among the DeLisser illustrations supplied by Stone are: "Under Sunset Rock, South Mountain;" "Cliff on South Mountain;" and "Fairy Spring, South Mountain." Kaaterskill Falls and its nearby Bastion Falls also received his attention.

Other artists appeared and reappeared as the decades of the nineteenth century moved onward. Some artists came to view, while others came to sketch and paint. The Palenville Art Colony, a yearly summer gathering of kindred spirits, had a lengthy history during the nineteenth century and deserves a more detailed study than given to date. Depending upon their lengths of stay and their financial resources, a variety of accommodations were available to these Hudson River artists and their successors. The Mountain House, after 1823, was one of the more convenient places for food and lodging, although the short season had its drawbacks. Some preferred the Laurel House practically atop of Kaaterskill Falls, while Brockett's in the Clove was a pre-Civil War facility. Few brought their families, although there were numerous farmsteads in the Kiskatom Valley willing to provide necessities at affordable prices.

As America prospered and traveling conditions improved, particularly after the Civil War, the touring public found the Catskill region to be a delightful summering experience. *Harper's Weekly* and *Harper's Monthly* were among the several magazines carrying artistic sketches to illustrate "description and travel" articles. Between the years 1866 and 1872, four individuals with superior sketching ability combined with a lighter touch of style came to the Mountain Top to create artistic impressions for publications: Thomas Nast, Fritz Meyer, Harry Fenn, and Winslow Homer. They were among a new breed of artists who had benefitted from the production of field sketches during the Civil War. Thomas Nast became, in time, a political cartoonist of national stature while Winslow Homer brought the watercolor to new heights of excellence. His impressions in that genre gained him an international reputation.

The July 21, 1866, issue of *Harper's Weekly* provided its readers with the opportunity to be amused and entertained by Thomas Nast's "Sketches Among the Catskill Mountains." Its double-page engraving of twenty-eight scenes and activities centered around the Mountain Top. Nast combined both humor and scenic appreciation. In addition to the predicaments of overly ambitious hikers and problems with excessively cumbersome trunks, there are captioned views—"Haines Falls," "Kaaterskill Falls," and "In the Woods."

For his *Catskill Mountain Album* (1869), Fritz Meyer created a series of individual scenes without the Nast humor. Here, we find cloves, waterfalls, the Mountain House, all above a bottom marginal outline of the Catskill range of mountains. These also were combined in a composite printing, one separate from the individual views in the album itself.

If Meyer's album was for the masses, William Cullen Bryant's *Picturesque America* was for the upper classes. It is regarded as the ultimate of such picture books. D. Appleton & Co. produced the American edition in two volumes between 1872 and 1874. An English edition in four volumes for ease in handling reached the market between 1894 and 1897. Harry Fenn produced the illustrations for the Catskill section.

The 1872 drawing "Kaaterskill Falls" by Winslow Homer illustrates interest in that genre. Having utilized the stairs, two young ladies, leaning on their souvenir walking sticks, are observing a male companion and his adventurous female partner attempting to reach and explore the cavern under the first section of the waterfall.

Commercial entrepreneurs, over the years, saw an opportunity for profit in producing single prints for framing, the Bartletts being a prime example. A close runner-up of cruder production were those from Currier and Ives. The undated *Catterskill Falls* depicts an almost overwhelming force of water falling from the two levels. The observation platform with its American flag and two figures at the mid-level section are part of the print's composition. *Scenery of the Catskills* is another Currier and Ives effort of uncertain date. Here the sedate hiking party is on North

Mountain, the Mountain House and the two lakes included.

The passage of time has brought about the loss of the Catskill Mountain House and the twin lakes have been combined into one single body of water. Yet much of this Mountain Top remains, the hiker superseding the artists, the campground the hotel. Scattered throughout the various states from the Atlantic to the Pacific's Hawaii, in museums, art galleries, and in private collections, is prominently displayed "the scenic grandeur" of the Mountain Top. It is an American heritage nonpareil.

Moby Dick

And there is a Catskill eagle in some souls that can alike dive down into the blackest gorges, and soar out of them again and become invisible in the sunny spaces. And even if he forever flies within the gorge, that gorge is in the mountains; so that even in his lowest swoop the mountain eagle is still higher than the other birds upon the plain, even though they soar.

Herman Melville

Rails to the Peaks

by William F. Helmer

The awed and apprehensive motorist negotiating the steep and winding road up the Kaaterskill Clove may find it hard to believe that at the very top, in the heart and at the height of the northern Catskills, two railroad systems maintained competing passenger stations. And yet, each and every summer season for many years, such was the case.

The year 1882 marked the arrival of the narrow-gauge Kaaterskill Railroad in the notch between North and South Mountains; ten years later, the Otis Elevating Railway began lifting passengers to the Catskill Mountain House ledge, less than a mile from the terminus of the Kaaterskill. The former approached the high country from the south, then west, from a connection with the Ulster & Delaware. The other scaled the mountain wall from the east, from a connection with the narrow-gauge Catskill Mountain Railway. Their rivalry continued until 1918 when the Otis abandoned its line, leaving the successors of the Kaaterskill to furnish service until the 1940 season, after which no more trains rumbled along the hillsides.

Railroads do not climb hills well. The expense of engineering, constructing, maintaining and operating a mountain railroad is tremendous. That two companies accepted the challenge and responsibility of pushing iron rails into these altitudes would seem to indicate a form of corporate insanity, whose infection had spread. Regardless of appearances, there were some very sound reasons that these lines were built and, for a time, prospered.

Resort rivalry was acute in the nineteenth century in the Catskills. The famous and fashionable Catskill Mountain House, while it enjoyed a privileged position in the Catskill hotel hierarchy, was soon but one of the many lodging places. The New York, Ontario & Western Railway was bringing swarms of summer visitors into the lower reaches of the Catskills, to the farm/boarding houses and new hotels opening in response to the greater accessibility given by this new line. Paralleling this route was the recently built Ulster & Delaware, linked at Kingston with the New York, West Shore & Buffalo. These two conduits offered a rapid all-rail route from New York City to the southern foothills of the Catskill vacation land.

The fear among the proprietors of the older hostelries in the upper reaches of Greene County was that their Ulster and Sullivan County rivals would profit at their expense. Particularly apprehensive was Charles L. Beach, owner of the Mountain House, whose customers faced a slow steamboat trip up the Hudson to the landing at Catskill village and then a fifteen-mile ordeal by stagecoach to the hotel. He also had to worry about a neighbor, George Harding, a Philadelphia lawyer who undertook erection of a luxurious resort facility on nearby South

Mountain. While Harding's Kaaterskill Hotel might attract many to the area, it might also draw away former Mountain House patrons.

Harding's advantage was assured when the offices of the Ulster & Delaware Railroad announced the formation of the Stony Clove & Catskill Mountain and Kaaterskill railroads, to hook up with the U & D main line at Phoenicia for the run to Hunter and to the Kaaterskill Hotel. This gave Harding a direct rail line to his clientele.

To meet this threat, Beach found allies in the steamboat companies, which shared his concern about the impact of railroads on the traveling public. Officers of the Hudson River Day Line and the Catskill Evening Line joined him in promoting and constructing the narrow-gauge Catskill Mountain Railroad, to connect the steamboat dock at the village of Catskill with Palenville at the foot of Kaaterskill Clove. There passengers from the boat transferred to the same familiar omnibuses, but for a much shorter trip than before. The smoother, faster ride on the little trains eliminated all but the short jaunt up the Mountain House Road.

Put into operation late in the summer of 1882, the Catskill Mountain Railway met some of the objections to the longer, slower Catskill village-to-mountaintop stage route. Despite these efforts, the Kaaterskill Hotel and the Kaaterskill Railroad (completed in 1883) still enjoyed the advantage.

To close the rail gap between the Mountain House and Palenville, Beach and his associates conceived and then built an unconventional sort of vertical rail line, operated by a stationery engine, cables, and attached passenger cars. The 1892 Otis Elevating was not only a marvel of engineering but an amusement ride, which drew the curious and the adventurous just for the novelty of the thing. It was a solution, a partial solution, to the problems with the Catskill Landing approach to the mountains. While it gave access to the venerable Mountain House, it did not give access to the newer Kaaterskill Hotel and the other inns beyond. Each of the two major hotels now had its own depot, separated by about a mile of scenery.

Realizing the desirability of a total mountaintop rail link, the two companies called a brief truce. If the Otis interests would lay the track from Otis Summit station to the depot at Kaaterskill, the Kaaterskill Railroad would furnish train service over that line. It was a kind of shotgun wedding, however, for the Otis operators had earlier warned that they were about to build another, new railroad from the Summit to Tannersville for the purpose of serving the "Resort Ridge" on the six-mile lane west from the incline.

The delicate "marriage" lasted for but a short time. In 1898 the parent Ulster & Delaware widened the gauge of its Kaaterskill branch to correspond with the main line, eliminating the need for a train change at the Phoenicia junction. This left the Catskill Mountain-Otis Elevating companies in a difficult situation. To preserve their narrow-gauge system and retain the traffic, the managers severed the Kaaterskill linkage and broke ground for an extension to Tannersville parallel to the existing line but on much inferior terrain. Thus the "Huckleberry," as the Catskill & Tannersville came to be known, was established.

These were good days for both businessman and traveler. The public had a multitude of choices of route and method of transportation to the prime Catskill resorts: by steamboat, by standard-gauge or narrow-gauge railway, and in almost infinite number of combinations. No one needed to return in the same way he came. And for the transportation companies and hotelkeepers, prospects were bright.

Up until the start of the Great War in 1914, the railroads did well, but thereafter they fell on bad days. The narrow-gauge Catskill Mountain lines (including the Otis and the Catskill & Tannersville) suffered most, for they were isolated from other sources of revenue and dependent upon the river connection. Increasing operating costs, decreasing numbers of steamboat travellers, popularity of the motor car, and the attractiveness of more remote vacation areas all led to the bankruptcy and dissolution of the narrow-gauge lines. They were gone by 1919, leaving the Ulster & Delaware Railroad to perform its smoky duties alone on the Catskill heights. In 1940 the U & D (by then the Catskill Mountain Branch of the New York Central) also withdrew from the mountaintop area, defeated at last by the internal combustion engine.

The freedom, the flexibility, and the convenience of the motor car contributed greatly to a change not only in transportation. Summer vacationers were no longer restricted to long stays in big hotels; they could zip about from motor court to motor court, or from tenting ground to tenting ground, drive all night or sleep in the car—the possibilities were astounding in their variety. The result was a decline of the entire mountaintop resort industry.

Today only traces remain of what was once a booming rail-transportation enterprise. Here and there may be found the relics treasured by the antiquarian—the rusted rail bolt or spike, the half-hidden bridge abutment, the converted railroad station, the overgrown embankment. It requires an effort of the imagination to hear the whistles again in the mountains, for the scattered remnants can only suggest the bustling life that once was there.

The Birth of the Kaaterskill

A legend that grew in the forest's hush
Slowly as tear-drops gather and gush,—
    It grew and grew,
From the pine-trees gathering a somber hue,
Till it seems a mere murmur out of the vast
Norwegian forests of the past

James Russell Lowell

Forest History of the Kaaterskill Region

by Michael Kudish

The Kaaterskill Region contains the widest diversity of plant species of any area of similar size in the Catskills. The reason for this is explained by the topography and soils. The abrupt change in elevation from about 500 feet on Kaaterskill High Peak, North Mountain, and Stoppel Point in as little distance as two miles creates a great shortening of the growing season. In addition, the contrast between deep, rich limestone and shale-origin soils at the base of the Escarpment and the acid shallow, rocky soils derived from sandstone and conglomerate at its crest creates vast differences in vegetation. In no other portion of the Catskills is the climate and soil contrast so striking as here.

It is this same abrupt change in elevation plus the scenic cloves, falls, lakes, and outlook ledges that has attracted so many visitors, writers, painters, and naturalists. The proximity of the

Hudson Valley, which was first settled in what is now Greene County in the mid-seventeenth century, has provided for three centuries of human observation and disturbance at the base of the Escarpment. This is a long period for any region in the United States. Activity above the Escarpment is almost as long-lived, having rapidly accelerated after the Revolutionary War.

Despite this long period of attention and human disturbance, the nature of the Kaaterskill region forest has not changed much since the seventeenth century! Although most of the huge trees are gone—early writings record white pine 5 years in diameter and hemlock 4 feet in diameter—the younger individuals now found are of the same species and probably exist in species proportions similar to the original forest. Many disturbances were and are temporary, the forest eventually returning to its original species composition within a century or two. Such return occurs following both human and naturally caused disturbances.

The importance of soil depth in shaping the vegetation of the Catskills has been emphasized in my recent work, *Catskills Soils and Forest History*, which was published earlier this year by The Catskill Center. I was barely aware of this important factor in 1971 when I completed my dissertation on the vegetational history of the Catskill high peaks. Only where a disturbance removes much soil can the vegetation which follows differ greatly from that of before. Soils inches thick on steep ledges will not and never have supported a forest. It is on these sites where the forest has not been able to invade since the end of the ice age that one or two alpine plants, the cinquefoil and mountain sandwort, have persisted.

The only previously abundant species no longer found is the American chestnut. Its elimination is not unique to the Kaaterskill region but occurred throughout the eastern United States, caused by a fungus blight accidentally introduced into New

York City in 1904. The blight struck the Kaaterskill region some time after World War I. The American chestnut grew only on the Escarpment to an elevation of about 2,500 feet, where it still exists today as stump sprouts, but rarely as mature trees.

What species constitute the forest of the Kaaterskill Region today? The southern Hudson Valley species which mix with the more northerly cousins on the Escarpment to about the 2500 foot level are oaks (red, white, and chestnut), hickories, pitch pine, black birch, and mountain laurel. The middle Catskills elevations, from about 1000 or 1500 feet up to about 3000 feet, harbor mostly a hemlock-white pine-northern hardwoods forest, consisting of mostly sugar maple, beech, and yellow birch. Some black cherry, white ash, basswood, and hop hornbeam also can be found. Finally, at the highest elevations above 3000 feet is the boreal spruce-fir forest with paper birch and mountain ash. On shallow soils and in swamps between 2000 and 3000 feet, spruce-fir forest occurs also where northern hardwoods cannot invade—hence the abundance around the lakes. Pioneer species which temporarily move in following disturbances are red (pin) cherry, aspens, sumac, and paper birch. Each forest zone has it corresponding ground cover, with some overlap, of course.

Many naturalists have studied the forests in the Kaaterskill region. Their early documentation is relevant to discussing the forest of today. Two of the most significant were John Bartram and James Pierce.

John Bartram's journey with his son, William, in September 1753 is described in detail by Alf Evers in his Catskill classic, *The Catskills from Wilderness to Woodstock*. Bartram's purpose was to collect balsam fir seeds around North and South Lake for the botanist Peter Collinson in England. (Bartram had been to the area in 1741 to study what he found "the greatest variety of uncommon trees and shrubs that I ever saw in such a compass of ground".) A guide led the Bartrams through a forest of spruce, hemlock, fir, beech, and white birch to Kaaterskill Falls. Bartram noted the soil was shallow in places but did not fully realize the importance of soil depth in determining the distribution of vegetation in the Catskills. He did not mention any signs of human activity or settlements around the lakes at the time of his visit.

Bartram's list, based on observations during his ascent of South Mountain, is included here. It is similar to the lists of other early naturalists and is indeed similar to a list which might be made today:

- pitch pine
- red pine
- white pine
- white spruce [This is unlikely;
    Bartram meant red spruce]
- fir
- sugar birch [black birch?]
- caprifolium [some viburnum?]
- march broad-leaved viburnum
- beech
- red oak
- chestnut oak [He called it "Prinus"]
- paper birch
- wild cherry
- ash
- honeysuckle
- opulus [highbush cranberry or
    maple leaved viburnum?]
- sweet service [juneberry]
- mountain maple
- striped maple
- willow
- purple spiraea [hardhack]
- laurel or ivy [probably mountain laurel]

•aralia spinosa [Aralia hispida?]

James Pierce, who explored the area in 1823, had an insight into the relationship between the forest and the environment uncommon for his time. The following passage seems to have been written a century ahead of its time, as Pierce's awareness of vegetational change with elevation and physiography is surprising:

> *Gradations of elevation on the mountain are in some degree marked by a change of vegetation both as it respects the species and periods of blossoming, and the maturity of fruit. The lower districts and the warm southern exposures or ravines exhibit trees and plants common to the Hudson River Valley: oak, chestnut, soft and hard maple, ash, and cherry, mingled with a few evergreens. On the peaks, on the northern cold sides of ranges, in moist shaded ravines, and elevated valleys, the trees and plants of the Green Mountains and northern part of New England occur. You see these thick groves of hemlock, spruce, balsam fir, pitch pine, mingled with hard maple, beach [sic], white and black birch, and cherry. The white pine is not observed on the eastern range of the Catskill Mountains, but is found in the valley of the Schoharie and adjacent hills of moderate elevation.*
>
> *Among the mountain shrubs, the blackberry, thimble berry [raspberry] and moose bush [Moosehead maple] are noted; the whortleberry [blueberry] is very abundant on the rocky summits, and is the favorite of bears. The plants of the mountain blossom much later than those of the valley and a botanist can collect plants of different latitudes, or which blossom at different periods in one day's research.*

Based on the preceding description , the early forest and the present one are quite similar.

The species similarity does not mean that the forests of the Kaaterskill region have been without change, however. Human activity in the area since the American Revolution has had its impact. To understand the forest as more than simply a species list, we need to examine the various factors that have influenced and shaped it into the form we find today.

Vegetational disturbances can be caused by people or they can be natural. Examples of the latter are wind blowdown, disease epidemics, lightning fires, landslides, extended droughts, etc. Such natural disturbances have been occurring since the forest invaded the Catskills following deglaciation, about 14,000 or 15,000 years ago. Much of this early natural disturbance we may never know. The examination of photographs, especially those taken in the nineteenth century, are very helpful, as are the writings of early naturalists who explored the Region before and up to the commencement of tannery operations in 1817.

The tanneries utilized the bark of hemlock trees to obtain the tannin needed to convert hides to usable leather. Sawmills, attracted by the availability of both forests and water power, also contributed to the depletion of the first growth forest in the region. Other uses of the Kaaterskill forest were for barrel hoops, Christmas trees, building materials, and furniture built at local factories.

We should realize that logging, barking, or fire are only temporary disturbances to a forest unless all or most soil is removed in the process. A well done, careful logging operation is a very minor and only temporary disturbance to a forest; once the stump rot and the skid roads grow over, evidence of logging is gone. But it is safe to say that in the last century, there was much less care taken and much more waste than at present.

Clearing for scenic views was another human disturbance. Several of the phographs and drawings found else where in this guide show the area around the Kaaterskill Hotel to be devoid of any large trees. The Hotel was set back from the Escarpment and its view of the Hudson Valley depended on the openness created in front of the huge building.

The effect upon the forests by recreationists cannot be overlooked, especially if these tourists were hiking in large numbers. Recreational disturbance appeared in the area about the time of the opening of the Catskill Mountain House in 1824 and grew to an all-time peak between 1882 and 1918—the railroad era. This kind of disturbance was mostly concentrated along trails, lookouts, and roads, with few hikers venturing forth bushwhacking.

Through the 1860's and probably up to 1881 when the Hotel Kaaterskill was built, most hikers were funneled along trails which diverged from the MountainHouse. Roland Van Zandt, author of *The Catskill Mountain House*, states that hikers had reached North Point by 1866. Before the 1860's, the Mary's Glen Trail was in use as an easier return to the Mountain House from points along North Mountain. Trails certainly ascended South Mountain so that hikers could enjoy views from the Palenville and other overlooks. Also, trails covered the area around and beneath Kaaterskill Falls. Staircases were already in existence down Kaaterskill Falls by 1854.

Beers, in his 1884 *History of Greene County*, stated that "Kaaterskill Park, as late as 1880, was in a wild and unbroken state dotted here and there only by the woodsman's path, or a small trail to some lookout." In

1881 the Hotel Kaaterskill was built followed by several burns: the forest was no longer unbroken! Lucy C. Lillie, writing in 1882, noted trail expansion (probably connections to the new Kaaterskill Hotel), and in 1894 a new path to South Mountain; in 1909 further trails were added and some old ones rebuilt.

Although the Kaaterskill region has had wide and varied use, several areas have had less vegetational disturbance than average. Two reasons might be the inaccessibility of these areas and the protective attitude of landowners. Charles Beach, owner of the Catskill Mountain House, favored no disturbance of the vegetation unless absolutely necessary. Despite his protective attitude toward Mountain House lands, disturbance in minor ways such as collecting plants as ornaments and souvenirs took place.

In 1971 I noted at least three small areas in the Kaaterskill Region that are most likely in original growth forest. True, hiking trails pass through these groves, but logging, bark peeling, and fires appear to have been absent for the last 300 years or more. E. G. West (who authored "The Escarpment Trail," also included in this guide) showed me a hemlock blazed by a surveyor in the 1820's. This hemlock stands in a grove of trees of similar great age along the creek between Kaaterskill and Bastian Falls. A second grove of trees 300 or more years old, including hemlock, occurs at Buttermilk Falls. Finally, at the 3000 or 3200 feet level on High Peak and Round Top, the forest certainly was never burned and most likely not logged.

Of all the action of significance to the forests of the area, probably the most telling for the future is the program of state acquisition for expansion of the Catskill Forest Preserve. The Forest Preserve was created by the State Legislature in the late nineteenth century to protect forest resources in both the Catskills and the Adirondacks from the ravages of commercial overuse and abuse then taking place. Once land located within the boundary of the Catskill Park—which is defined on state maps by a blue line boundary and encompasses all of the Kaaterskill region—is purchased for forest preserve purposes, it falls into the "forever wild" category and cannot be logged or otherwise commercially exploited. Any lands acquired by the State of New York as first growth will remain as first growth, which protection extends to the above noted 300-year old groves, while cut-over lands are permitted to regenerate. With the 1979 State acquisition of the 3500-acre Camp Harriman property in East Jewett, the entire Escarpment is protected by "forever wild" status.

KAATERSKILL STATION.

THE LEMON SQUEEZER, SOUTH MOUNTAIN

PUDDING-STONE HALL, SOUTH MOUNTAIN.

FAT MAN'S MISERY.

uvenir of the Catskill Mountains" manufactured by Christhom Bros., Portland, ME,
nufacturers of Charles Frey's original *Souvenir Albums of all American and Canadian Cities*
es. *Collection of Justine and Hillard Hommel.*

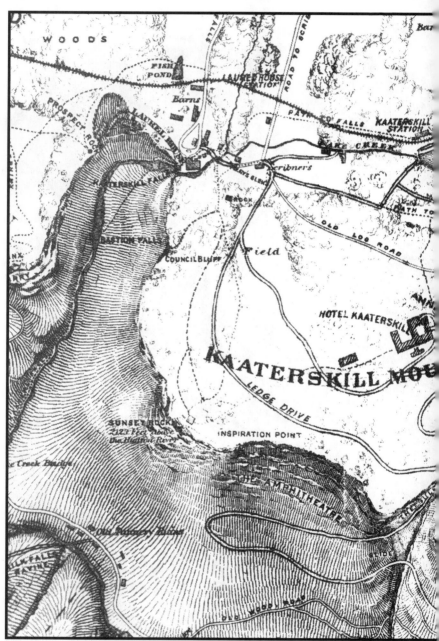

The Pine Orchard/Kaaterskill Clove area. Detail of map from Van Loan's *Catskill Mountain Guide*, New York, 1897, page 45.

"Souvenir of the Catskill Mountains" manufactured by Christhom Bros., Portland, ME, manufacturers of Charles Frey's original *Souvenir Albums of all American and Canadian Cities* series. *Collection of Justine and Hillard Hommel.*

The Catskill Mountain House, North and South Lakes and the Hotel Kaaterskill, from North Mountain. Photo by Herman Bickleman. *Collection of Estate of Roland Van Zandt.*

Newman's Ledge on the trail to North Mountain. Approximately 2700 feet above the Hudson River. Photo by Roland Van Zandt.

Sunset Rock, Kaaterskill Clove. Visitors pose for the cameraman along the eastern rim of the Clove, a favorite spot for tourists and artists, depicted in a number of Hudson River School paintings. Photo circa 1860, photographer unknown. *Collection of Justine and Hillard Hommel.*

ing South from South Mountain, by Harry Fenn, from an engraving by W.A. Cranston in
ıresque America, William Cullen Bryant, Ed., Vol.II, page 532. *Collection of Justine and Hillard*
ımel.

Alligator Rock, near South Lake. Photo by W.A. Jenner, landscape photographer, Windham, N *Collection of the Mountain Top Historical Society.*

Bluestone quarry on Prospect Mountain, near Sphinx Rock, Kaaterskill Clove. Photo by Alden Ticefeldt, Chichester, NY. *Collection of Haines Falls Free Library.*

ee growing around rock in Kaaterskill Clove. Photo circa 1975. *Photo by Bob Gildersleeve.*

Second Ledge on South Mountain Path, from Van Loan's *Catskill Mountain Guide*, 1879. Collection of Justine and Hillard Hommel.

r the Falls, Catskill Mountains, by Winslow Homer, published in *Harper's Weekly*, September 872. *Collection of the Estate of Roland Van Zandt.*

THE KATZ-KILLS IN WINTER.
Bastion Falls.

inted from lithograph by Currier & Ives. *Collection of Justine and Hillard Hommel.*

"The Ascent t o Kaaterskill Falls."

"Their Pilgrimage", Harper's Magazine, Vol.LXXII, December 1885 - May 1886. *Collection of Just and Hillard Hommel.*

y's Glen near Laurel House" from *Land of Rip Van Winkle. A Tour Through the Romantic Parts of atskills. Its Legends and Traditions*, by A.E.P. Searing, published by E. Heinemann, 1891. *tion of Justine and Hillard Hommel.*

r Pilgrimage" from *Harper's Magazine*, Vol.LXXII, December 1885 - May 1886. *Collection of e and Hillard Hommel.*

The Catterskill Fall (from below), by William Henry Bartlett, 1838. From *American Scenery*. Collec
of Deborah Allen.

Otis Elevating Railway, circa 1903. The Otis ran from Palenville to summit station near
th Lake and the Catskill Mountain House, a rise of 1,630 feet. *Collection of Justine and Hillard*
mel.

The Otis Elevating Railroad. Detroit Photographic Co., 1902. Library of Congress. *Collection of Haines Falls Free Library.*

Kaaterskill Station. Photo circa 1900-1910. Library of Congress. *Collection of Haines Falls Free Library.*

nes Corners Station (Catskill & Tannersville Narrow-Gauge Railroad). Library of Congress. *ection of Justine and Hillard Hommel.*

nes Corners, later called Haines Falls. Catskill & Tannersville (narrow gauge) Railroad ion in the foreground. The Ulster & Delaware Railroad Station in the background. Circa 0. Postcard from painting by Robert Skiba. *Collection of Mountain Top Historical Society.*

Huckleberry Railroad, Haines Corners, Catskill, Mts.

No. 2 engine, Catskill & Tannersville (narrow gauge) Railroad, known locally as "The Huckle berry." *Collection of The Haines Falls Free Library.*

urel House and Kaaterskill Falls. Photo circa 1900-1910. Library of Congress. *Collection of ines Falls Free Library.*

rom Van Loan's *Catskill Mountain Guide,* 1879. *Collection of Justine and Hillard Hommel.*

The Hotel Kaaterskill from Boulder Rock. Detroit Photographic Co., 1902. Library of Congress. *Collection of Haines Falls Free Library.*

Parlor, Hotel Kaaterskill, Catskill Mts.

PC 566 Copyright, 1909, by Samuel E. Rusk, Haines Falls, N. Y. — Germany

The Hotel Kaaterskill parlor. Postcard. Photo by Samuel E. Rusk. *Collection of Haines Falls Free Library.*

...w of the Mountain House, by William Henry Bartlett, 1839. From *American Scenery. Collection of ...untain Top Historical Society.*

...enery of the Catskills, unsigned, undated print by Currier & Ives. *Collection of Estate of Roland ...an Zandt.*

In Front of the old Catskill Mountain House.   Catskill Mountains, N. Y.

"In Front of the Old Catskill Mountain House." Postcard. Published by American News Co., NY, circa 1895. *Collection of Haines Falls Free Library.*

The burning of the Catskill Mountain House by the New York State Conservation Department on Friday, January 25, 1993, 6:00 am. *Collection of the Estate of Edward G. West.*

Faun-Fa
A Story of the
Catskill Mountains

But the grandest sight of all,
Was the mountain waterfall.
Where a wandering streamlet led,
From the lake, to where, o'erhead,
Here the mighty hills divide,
In an archway deep and wide,
Taking thence a sudden leap,
Down into the ravine deep.

Clara Ingersoll Waring

Kaaterskill Lodgings

by Justine L. Hommel

In the area covered by this guide, there were three famous hotels—the Catskill Mountain House, the Hotel Kaaterskill, and the Laurel House, and Glen Mary Cottage, a boarding house. All four structures are gone now, but contributed in their own way to the fame of North and South Mountains, North and South Lakes, the Kaaterskill Falls and Ravine.

Detailed accounts and books have been written about them. Paintings, sketches and photographs depict them in all the stages of their existence. The following accounts are intended as vignettes of these unique lodgings, not as historical pieces. It is hoped that these introductions will persuade the reader to consult Rockwell, Longstreth, Vedder, Van Zandt, Evers, Best, Helmer, and the many others who have prepared extensive works about these hotels. It is the fascination, love and concern of these authors and historians that have preserved the history and importance of these lodgings which complemented the extraordinary beauty of their natural settings, a beauty that remains today long after the hotels themselves.

The Catskill Mountain House

Is it absurd to suggest that a hotel could acquire a human personality in its 160 years of operation? Telling of the Catskill Mountain House, one is struck by the emotional appeal and drama that always surrounded it. From its humble origin until the last days of its existence, people worried about it and watched it carefully as one watches a dear friend or relative. Its 160 years might be compared to the life of a person, from its glowing, beautiful youth until its ruinous, painful old age.

Opened in 1823, the Catskill Mountain House immediately commanded the Hudson River and its valley, and the Catskill Mountains. Its white beauty reached out from its rock ledge at Pine Orchard, enticing the world and inviting all to visit; and a large part of the world did!

As is the case in reaching many of the world's most beautiful spots, one had to pay a price. The journey by stage was rough and agonizing. Each early writer described in detail the trip through the dangerous ravine below. After the first steep climb, the road leveled off for a bit. At this point the majestic dwelling on the cliff high above came into view. Perhaps the painting called *View of the Catskill Mountain House, New York* by Thomas Cole, c.1828, most clearly depicts the exhilaration and excitement of the viewer first seeing the Mountain House from that point.

Lodgings

The Catskill Mountain House became a showplace under the ownership and management of the Beach family. It had elegance and style, and held the fashionable society of the day at its command. Writers, authors, painters, and the rich and famous came to stroll on the 140-foot front plaza. Thirteen Corinthian columns were added about 1845, giving it a Grecian elegance and adding stature to its predominance.

Bayard Taylor, the nineteenth century author and translator, reported "the guests are a rather quiet company. Several entire families were quartered there for the season. Still it afforded a wonderful privacy. You would not have guessed the number of guests if you had not seen them at the table." During the day, each person sought his own pleasure. Hiking was an important part of any visit to the Catskills. Extensive trails, famous views and lookouts fanned out from the Mountain House in all directions. A stroll toward South Lake for a boat ride offered the opportunity to visit Alligator Rock. (Postcards produced for the Kaaterskill Hotel often called the same rock, Crocodile or Whale's Mouth). Many contented themselves in rocking chairs watching the steamboats on the Hudson below.

The Beach family tenacity, single-mindedness and resolute firmness, coupled with a certain moral thinking, was transferred to the Catskill Mountain House in the ninety-one years under their management. The characteristics of its "middle age" were established. One example was the quiet, religious observances of Sunday beginning with an eleven o'clock service and frequently followed in the afternoon or evening by other theologically related events. In spite of, or perhaps because of, this somber approach, younger guests often felt a need to release their inhibitions. Parties were popular and frequent, as were dances, concerts, bowling, billiards, tennis, and other popular activities of the day.

Another antiquated ritual that persisted concerned the dining room. Meals were always served at a specific time, and all guests received the same meal. The food, wines, and service were excellent in quality. In an age when individual tastes were catered to, however, Mr. Beach refused to vary from his policies. This brought him into conflict with one important guest, Mr. George Harding, and led to the establishment of a major competitor to the Mountain House, as detailed in a later section of this article.

The Catskill Mountain House occasionally teetered on financial instability but managed to survive one way or another. It exhibited elegance and held a place of superiority among resorts throughout most of the nineteenth century. Its famous guests included such people as General Sherman, Presidents Arthur and Grant, Maude Adams, Hamilton Garland and Tyrone Power, to mention a few. And because of its unique character and special clientele the Mountain House seized its guests over the years in a kind of emotional entanglement. It courted them as a lover, created moods of excitement, inspiration and endearment, and held fast. It was a part of the mystique that made it almost human.

The Beach family owned the stagecoach which brought its guests to the summit. Charles L. Beach resisted the movement toward railroads on the premise that the Catskills were already too accessible. In his view, the railroad would bring undesirable people, specifically the poor and middle-class. But Beach could not hold back the appearance of the railroads. They came and with them the accessibility that Beach feared, perhaps rightly for his hotel. With increased competition from newer hotels and boarding houses throughout the Catskills, the glorious age of the great mansion passed, and the Catskill Mountain House slowly moved from the height of its attractiveness to old age.

Eventually, the lofty temple on the hill began to show signs of age—and weariness. People still went there, but they were no longer the famous and fashionable. They were not of the social standing of those "400 paying guests" who had filled the north and south wing additions in the 1850's and 1870's.

Balls and concerts were held as in the past. Advertisements boasted of pure air, pure water, and grand views, and one claimed "absolute freedom from malaria." But the hotel tried to adapt to changes. There were many new features, electric lights, telephones, and a social director! It was all ready and waiting.

Reluctantly, Charles Beach also realized that a more direct rail connection to his Mountain House was necessary. So he conceived the idea of the Otis Elevating Railroad, connecting the narrow-gauge railroad, which ran from Catskill to Palenville, to his hotel. The Otis was a cable system with two cars. It had a station in Palenville and a second at the summit behind North Lake, just a short distance from the Mountain House. The elevated railroad was installed down the face of the mountain. It was about 7,000 feet long and carried passengers 1,600 feet up the face of the Wall of Manitou. It was built, and the rails installed in thirteen months, a remarkable engineering feat.

When Charles Beach died in 1902, the Catskill Mountain House was reaching old age. His sons Charles and George H. became the owners. George's daughter, Mary, was married to John Van Wagonen in an elaborate ceremony in 1911. Guests sailed up the Hudson by river boat, took the train from Catskill Landing, and then boarded the

Otis Incline to the Catskill Mountain House. A spotlight, which signalled messages to the night boats on the river, was mounted on the ledge. It was a very grand affair. The newlyweds were given two thousand acres of Mountain House land as a wedding present.

The younger Charles Beach died in 1913. It was about this time that the mountain tourist trade began to undergo a change. America had become motorized. Behind the wheels of their own cars and no longer dependent upon public transportation, tourists were driving to visit all sorts of new places, leaving behind the Catskill Mountain hotels. The decline was slow, the result of many influences and changes.

When George H. Beach died in 1918, John Van Wagonen became the manager of the hotel, which was now nearly a century old. The Catskill Mountain House had survived times of national economic reversals, but the Great Depression of the 1930's was too great a blow. During the 1920's and early 1930's it had been the policy of the hotel to borrow money in the spring from the Mountain National Bank in Tannersville in order to get the summer season underway. The loan would then be repaid after a successful season. The seasons became less successful and occasionally it was not possible to repay the full loan. Still additional loans were obtained.

In 1930, John Van Wagonen sold the two thousand acres which had been a wedding present, plus 197.93 acres to the State of New York for $12 per acre. This, with work done by the Civilian Conservation Corps, was the origin of North Lake Campsite.

Milo Claude Moseman, who was president of the Mountain National Bank, had once been a bellhop at the Mountain House. He felt a strong attachment to the famous hotel and was convinced that it would one day return to its glory years. When the bank holiday occurred in 1933, Claude Moseman was charged with misappropriation of the bank's funds. With the help of lawyer, Daniel H. Pryor of Albany and "the people of Tannersville who would trust him with their last dollar," he was able to avoid imprisonment. Eventually, he and Clyde Gardiner of Saugerties became owners of the Catskill Mountain House.

The hotel continued to function. It was leased to Jacob, Eli, and David Andron, who changed the name to Andron's Mountain House with a Kosher cuisine and a Jewish clientele. With the outbreak of World War II, the Androns did not renew their lease. It opened for the last time in the summer of 1942 under the management of Claude Moseman. The effort proved a complete failure and its doors closed forever.

The New York State Department of Conservation wanted to expand the campsite at North Lake and began negotiating with Moseman for the purchase of additional land near North and South Lake. In 1942, the State offered $30,000 but Moseman wanted $35,000. A compromise was reached at $32,500. Moseman was in Albany, about to sign the papers, when the then head of Land Acquisitions, Arthur Hopkins, commented, "Well, I guess you're glad to get rid of that white elephant." Moseman put down his pen and left the room, breaking off all negotiations forever.

The great white structure stood on its rock ledge and deteriorated. Its death was slow and painful. In 1950, a hurricane destroyed at least half of its columns. Rumors of efforts to save the Mountain House circulated for more than ten years.

In a move to raise money, Moseman (who had become sole owner) sold a parcel of land to Rip's Retreat. This was an early theme park containing authentic replicas of Hudson Valley Dutch houses. Here early crafts were demonstrated and a puppet show depicting the Rip Van Winkle story was staged. There were several other attractions including, of course, Rip Van Winkle and his dog, Wolf.

In an effort to save the central part of the house, Moseman decided to remove the north and south wings. His hope to obtain money from the salvage did not materialize. The devastation after the salvage operation was unbelievable. Viewing it was a sad and depressing sight. What remained of the once beautiful columns showed an unwillingness to continue supporting the broken, unsteady giant. The portico was propped up with sticks. Its ravished hulk cried out in agony. The wind howled through its emptiness like a death rattle. From deep within there were unreal sounds, often followed by an unnatural, poignant silence. It was very clear that this giant of by-gone years was dying.

Milo Claude Moseman died in 1958 leaving, as Roland Van Zandt suggests in his book, *The Catskill Mountain House*, "the wreckage of his dreams on the shattered height of Pine Orchard."

In 1961, Rip's Retreat was sold at auction, purchased by the Nature Conservancy and turned over to the State of New York. The remaining property, which had been sold by Moseman's heirs to Carpathian Vacation Camp, Inc., and the Catskill Mountain House was obtained by the Conservation Department on April 9, 1962. Early in the morning, before daylight on January 23, 1963, the Mountain House died, intentionally destroyed by fire. When the embers died, there was nothing left on the ledge next to the long, straight scar running from top to bottom of the Wall of Manitou marking what was once the Otis Incline.

Only memories of The Great White Mansion and the Golden Era of the Catskills remain. Old timers who look up on a moonlit night at the spot where the great hotel once stood can almost see it standing there, and when they listen, strains of the music once heard below seem to be echoing through the hills.

Hotel Kaaterskill

The story of George Harding's reason for building the stupendous Hotel Kaaterskill is a tale which has been told often with many embellishments added over the century of telling. The story most accepted is what Alf Evers refers to in his classic Catskill history *The Catskills: From Wilderness to Woodstock* as "The Fried Chicken War."

George Harding was a wealthy patent lawyer from Philadelphia. As had been their habit in previous summers, the Harding family was vacationing at the Catskill Mountain House in the summer of 1880. Both Mrs. Harding and her daughter Emily were ailing and were on restricted diets. When a request was made for fried chicken for Emily, the waiter refused. His refusal was upheld by Charles Beach who ultimately suggested sarcastically that Mr. Harding might build his own hotel if he disagreed with the policies of the Catskill Mountain House. Harding, who claimed to have spent $4,000 a year at the hotel, decided to do just that! The site he chose was about a mile away on the top of South Mountain.

Meeting Beach's challenge, George Harding resolved that he would build and open the "largest woodframe hotel in the world" by June 1881. The site was intentionally located 245 feet above the Mountain House, as its advertisements later never failed to point out. Harding, however, failed to realize that the hotel's position exposed it to severe winds from all directions, necessitating its being anchored by long rods driven into the flat rock bed on which it stood. Longstreth, in his 1918 book, *The Catskills*, commented: "We came to a path that took us up to the Kaaterskill House, a mammoth hotel set near the summit of this mountain. It was hawsered to the rocks as was the Overlook, and presented an invitation to the heavy gusts that hurled themselves as yet not in vain upon its white hulk."

An army of 700 workmen was hired to build the Hotel Kaaterskill. In the great haste to accomplish an 1881 opening, careless lack of supervision resulted in waste and extravagance. Building during the winter of 1800-1881 was made difficult by a multitude of problems. First and foremost was the weather, with 3 feet of snow and temperatures of 10^0 below zero. All of the material had to be hauled by horse and wagon from the banks of the Hudson. Throughout the winter, building materials and furnishings arrived at the new site. It was necessary to build a road up the steep side of South Mountain. Consultations were held with some of the country's most noted railroad engineers, who doubted if it could be built. The plans they submitted were found to be too costly and impractical. In the end, Edward Dibble and Collins Hyser of Platte Clove were hired, and their logic and knowledge produced a remarkable road.

According to a promotional publication, the hotel had four hundred rooms in its first year of operation. Fifty of those had their own separate bathrooms. The promise of the following year was that there would be over one hundred more, with additional sleeping rooms, making it possible to accommodate twelve hundred guests. The construction of a "magnificent new" building at the north end of the earlier building, to be joined by a metal walkway, would make this a reality. "The whole length of the first floor," according to the brochure, "is an immense lecture-room nearly two hundred feet in length where the large assemblies can meet..." Other special features included "sweetest water from a limpid mountain lake three thousand feet above the sea," electric bells, telephones, gas lights within and electric lamps without. The ceilings were handsomely frescoed, while "all the metal work in sight is either bronze or nickel plate." Spacious stables were built to house over one hundred horses and innumerable carriages.

If one had any doubts of the authenticity of the animosity between Harding and Beach, a glance at the early Kaaterskill promotional material would verify their rivalry. On one page telling of hikes in the area, mention is made of a road leading to the "old Mountain House." The text quickly moves on with no other explanation. Sketches illustrating the text are carefully framed to exclude the Mountain House, as is the case in a view from North Mountain showing the Hotel Kaaterskill prominently in the distance, with no indication of the Mountain House on the ledge it had occupied for 60 years.

The Hotel Kaaterskill courted a more worldly clientele than did the Mountain House. Its gossipy little newspaper, *The Kaaterskill*, concerned itself with the names, professions, and home locations of current guests, and the clothes and jewels worn by them to the Grand Ball or the concerts. A report of the promenade on the long, expansive piazzas treated it as the social event of the season.

The advertisements called the Hotel Kaaterskill the largest mountain hotel in the world, located 3,000 feet (actually 2,480) above sea level, commanding a sixty-mile view of the Hudson River, with accommodations for 900 people. A Hudson man who had worked on the hotel claimed the building measured 2,044 feet around the outside and had 1,014 rooms for guests. Other specialties of the house were: baths, closets, gas, elevators, and later, telephones in every room—every modern convenience! A unique feature of the Kaaterskill was the Northern Lights Room, which offered a spectacular view of that phenomenon. It was said that the management was not averse to producing an artificial display when nature failed to supply the real thing.

In 1890 only half of the rooms were filled and Harding's hotel was losing money. The arrival of the railroads and the Otis Incline brought renewed visitor interest in the Catskills. In the long run, however, the reduction of travel time to reach the Kaaterskill also opened up the opportunity for short excursions and week-end vacations, contributing greatly to the passing of the era of huge hotels.

The Hotel Kaaterskill passed through three generations of Hardings and was eventually sold to Harry Tannenbaum in the early 1920's. Under the new management, its guests were mostly Jewish. Tannenbaum renovated the hotel and had a successful and profitable season in 1924. The hotel closed after Labor Day, leaving only six employees in the huge building. (Mr. Tannenbaum was in New Jersey recuperating from an operation.)

The fire that destroyed the Kaaterskill began at about 7 p. m. on September 8, 1924. It started in the kitchen from grease used in making soap and spread wildly through the wooden structure. The drafts of the great halls and the winds of South Mountain fanned the flames. The fire could be seen for miles, with one report from 65 miles away.

People in all the surrounding towns and villages saw flames shooting into the air with fountains of sparks and fire. A local resident, Goldye Slutzky, remembers having seen the fire as a child and vividly recalls burning window curtains flying outward from hundreds of windows. The huge hotel was quickly consumed.

Firemen from Haines Falls and Tannersville found it impossible to arrest the progress of the fire in the tinder-dry building. Instead, they turned their attention to helping the local police handle the crowds as thousands of nearby residents and late-summer guests jammed the roads leading to the fire. The accidental fire was an unknowing precursor of the purposely kindled fate that awaited the Catskill Mountain House almost 40 years in the future. At the time, however, it only clearly marked the end of an era, and avoided for the Kaaterskill the slow, painful deterioration that the other grand hotel was to experience.

The Laurel House

Peter Schutt came to the Kaaterskill Falls in 1824 and first built a log-cabin inn. He then built a dam upstream of the falls, giving him control of the water flow. The water was released for a fee. He built an observation deck overlooking the Falls, and it is said that those visiting the natural amphitheater below could have a lunch and a bottle of Champagne lowered from the platform above.

The demand for tourist accommodations near the Mountain House was increasing each year. But not every traveler was seeking the expensive and elaborate services offered by the Mountain House. It was elegant and the people who stayed there maintained the sophisticated formalities of their city life which others wanted to escape. Peter Schutt became aware of the need for more rooms near the Falls and decided in 1850 to build a boarding house. It was a simple, ordinary-type building, running parallel to Lake Creek, where as many as fifty persons could find rooms.

The Laurel House was unpretentious—a comfortable resort home for the average family. Lodging was for the middle class at half the price of the Mountain House—$1.25 per day. Charles Rockwell pointed out in his book, *The Catskill Mountains*, that guests of the Schutts could remain much after the summer season. The atmosphere was relaxed and pleasant. Artists and writers who gave lavishly glowing accounts of the Kaaterskill Falls and its frozen ice castles were among those who stayed at the Laurel House. Their writings and paintings are continuous reminders of the exquisite beauty of the area.

In the building and expansion of hotels and boarding houses in the Catskills that reached a peak shortly after the Civil War, an extension of 50 x 50 feet was added to the Laurel House. It lacked any distinctive features to lift it above the ordinary building. Then, sometime between 1879 and 1884, a complete change occurred. A large Victorian wing, measuring 40 x 125 feet, was built at right angles to the old building, adding charm and character to the house and making it totally a part of its time and era. It now had over 600 feet of piazzas, with balconies tucked behind its colonnades. The building was four stories high with a basement, and was crowned with a stylish cupola. Improvements such as gas, hot and cold baths, electric bells, etc. were a part of the expansion.

Lodgings

Jacob L. Schutt, Peter's son, became the proprietor. By 1884, the Laurel House claimed to rival the best hotels with its fine food, wines, and quiet grandeur. Still, it continued to attract a middle-class clientele. The Laurel House managed to survive, but never enjoyed great prosperity. On various occasions, its future seemed doubtful. It was sold at auction in 1900 to Jacob Fromer. In the early part of the century, there were many guests of German extraction, to be followed by what was referred to as a "mixed clientele." In 1920 it was sold to Bunting and Bernstein and joined the ranks of Jewish hotels in the Catskills. It was sold in 1954 to two sisters, Virginia Cardinale and Carmela Carella, who offered Italian-American cuisine. Their efforts to continue to operate the house which had been built more than a century before failed. They sold the Laurel House and 93 acres of land to the State of New York. The doors closed to the public for the last time on August 15, 1965. An auction was held and the contents sold.

On February 27, 1967, the first sign of the deliberate fire set by the Conservation Department appeared as a thin spiral of smoke near the cupola and, like its two grander neighbors, was reduced to ashes. The Laurel House will be remembered fondly as the guardian of the Falls at the top of the beautiful Kaaterskill Ravine.

Glen Mary Cottage

Ira and Mary Scribner built their small cottage in 1844 near Lake Creek close to the sawmill of Silas Scribner, Ira's father. It was Silas Scribner who sold a large tract of land in the area of South Lake to the Catskill Mountain Association, which built the hotel that later became the famous Catskill Mountain House. Ironically, in 1880 Ira sold the land on the top of South Mountain to George Harding so that he might build the only real competition the Mountain House knew. "Taking in boarders" was probably not exactly what the Scribners had in mind when they built their home. It offered no view of the spectacular Kaaterskill Ravine. Their business began almost by accident. In an era long before the advent of telephones, it was not uncommon for chance visitors to the Mountain House to be disappointed in finding all rooms occupied. The Glen Mary Cottage, named after Mrs. Scribner, became host to the overflow. Mary Scribner set a good table, kept a simple, clean house and charged very reasonable rates. Additions were made later, and Glen Mary Cottage gave many a weary traveler a resting place over the many years of its existence.

According to Alf Evers, referring again to his work *The Catskills: From Wilderness to Woodstock,* David Henry Thoreau and William Ellery Channing probably spent the night with the Scribners in 1844. They were undoubtedly the most illustrious persons to have shared the Scribners' board.

The sawmill and its dam provided a little extra money to the Scribner family in the form of a kind of "by product"—the waterfalls. They were able to control the water flowing over the 260 foot drop of the Kaaterskill by releases from the dam, for a price. That part of the business was later terminated when the Schutts built their dam close to the brink of the falls.

The area today offers no clue as to where the Glen Mary Cottage stood. Old maps indicate its location to have been at the end of what is now Schutt Road, just across the creek. Bulldozers have removed all evidence of its existence. A small part of the wall of the sawmill is still standing—precariously! At this point at Lake Creek, there is a strange and beautiful sense of quiet and loveliness, coupled with the urgency of the water as it seeks the most direct route to the Kaaterskill Falls and the canyon floor below. Standing there, one's attention is held by the immensity of the two rocks across the stream from the old foundation site—their presence marking the history of the spot they have held from the time of the glacier.

A ride of some three miles brought us as close as might be to the spot, the Falls, and a walk of as many hundred yards presented to view a scene as well suited for a witch's festival as any spot in the old world.

Tyrone Power

The Escarpment Trail

by Edward G. West

Of all the hundreds of miles in the Catskill Trail System, the Escarpment Trail is perhaps the most remarkable. It stretches along the northeastern escarpment of the Catskills, from Bastion Falls on Kaaterskill Creek at Route 23A to Route 23 at East Windham, a distance of 24 miles. In its entire length it does not cross a highway. Another striking feature is that parts of the trail are more than 150 years old, as evidenced by initials and dates carved in ledges along its length. I'd like to take you on a hike along this unique and historic footpath, where as Wallace Bruce wrote,

> *...Manitou once lived and reigned,*
> *Great Spirit of a race gone by,*
> *and Ontiora lies enchained*
> *With face uplifted to the sky.*

We'll start from Route 23A, at the top of the Kaaterskill Clove. In the first six or seven miles we will skirt along the top of the Great Wall of Manitou and traverse some of the most spectacular scenery found anywhere in the world, and among scenes made famous by historical and legendary events. For the first half mile, the trail follows the Kaaterskill Creek* upstream, which water forms the boundary between the Hardenbergh Patent and the State Land Tract, up to the foot of the Kaaterskill Falls, the highest waterfall in the East. The Falls are two hundred-sixty feet high, some twenty feet higher than Niagara.

These are the falls James Fenimore Cooper, in *The Pioneers*, has Natty Bumpo or Leather Stocking describe to Edwards. On the top of the Falls stood the old Laurel House. One can pass with ease behind the upper fall, but don't try it in winter under ice conditions.

And don't try to cross the stream just above the Falls at any time. The rocks are slippery and several people have slipped over the Falls in recent years. In the ledge just north of the upper fall is an interesting inscription carved more than a hundred years ago to the memory of a brave little dog who lost his life in the falls.

Passing on along the trail, we come to a white marble slab set in a stone monument, erected by the people of Twilight Park to mark the spot where Frank D. Layman lost his life on August 10, 1900 while fighting a forest fire. From here we can see our car where we parked it down on the Molly Smith Lookout Point on Route 23A.

Just above the Layman Monument is a fine lookout with a panoramic view of the Kaaterskill Clove. To the right, we see Haines Falls, Santa Cruz Ravine, Wild Cat Ravine, and across the clove High Peak and Round Top.

Editor's Note: Mr. West prefered the designation "Kaaterskill Creek" for this stream, a name also listed on various state maps. A map of 1876 and other sources, however, refer to the creek as Lake Creek, as it is known today by local residents.

Farther to the right, we can see the Hunter Mountain fire tower.

After brief stops for rest and to enjoy the impressive views at Sunset Rock (there is another Sunset Rock on North Mountain which we will also see), Inspiration Point and Bellevue Outlook, we come to the top of South Mountain. This is the site of the Kaaterskill Hotel, which was the largest mountain hotel and in its day the largest frame building in the world. It was built in 1881 by George Harding, a Philadelphia millionaire, to satisfy a grudge against Charles Beach, proprietor of the Catskill Mountain House, over a refusal by Mr. Beach to serve chicken to Mr. Harding's daughter. In September of 1924 this magnificent structure burned to the ground.

From the site of the Kaaterskill Hotel, we follow one of the old Harding carriage roads to a point near Boulder Rock, a round cobble on the edge of the cliff. The carriage road ends near this point as did the 150-year-old trail from the Catskill Mountain House. In fact, this boulder sat precisely on the line dividing the Kaaterskill and Mountain House properties. It doesn't matter now. The fried chicken war is long since over and both properties now belong to the State of New York as part of the Forest Preserve.

From Boulder Rock a trail somewhat in need of use and maintenance extends down the Ridge to Palenville Overlook, another scenic area in its own right. The Boulder Rock area deserves more than just a casual glance in passing through. In 1876 Walton Van Loan made a map of the Mountain House area on which he shows in considerable detail the foot paths and features of this part of South Mountain. There are so many interesting rock formations and things to see and ponder that one easily can spend a full day or more here, as I have on more than one occasion, following the trails around the edge of the swamp past Star

Rock, the Fairy Spring, through the Lemon Squeezer and Druid Rocks (where one can get down the high ledge if desired) and returning past Eagle Rock, the Sphinx, and the Slide.

It was in this area, and that of Pine Orchard, where botanist John Bartram and his son William came in 1753 to gather seeds and specimens of Balsam Fir to be sent to England and planted on the estates of the English aristocracy. In 1844, prior to his residence at Walden Pond, Henry David Thoreau visited the area and stayed with a sawmiller above Kaaterskill Falls.

It is only a few minutes walk from Boulder Rock to where the trail goes down a cleft in the ledge, one of only two or three places where one can easily get down.

Looking around, you'll notice rocks laid up to support and "level up" the trail, probably to make it easier for the ladies of the previous century, with their hoop skirts, to traverse the grade.

In another few minutes, and a little farther down, we break out into the clearing where the world-famous Catskill Mountain House stood. Built in 1823 and standing in all its glory on this high cliff overlooking the Hudson Valley, it could be seen from the Highlands of the Hudson almost to Albany. Gleaming white against the mountain top, its thirteen Corinthian columns represented the thirteen original colonies. Passengers on the Day Line boats and on the trains that skirted the river banks always looked for it. The night boat's search lights picked it up and the salute was returned by the searchlights mounted in front of the hotel.

The Catskill Mountain House had as its guests important people from across the world, including presidents of the United States and royalty from Europe. But its era came to an end in a sad story I will leave for another time. Suffice it to say the hotel became a desiccated ruin when on January 25, 1963 at 6:00 AM, before daylight and with a new fall of snow, the New York State Conservation Department applied a well-placed match.

As a tribute to the grand hotel, I should like to quote the last few sentences from Dr. Roland Van Zandt's excellent book, *The Catskill Mountain House*:

> *An hour later as the eastern sky grew luminous with departing star and planet, a monstrous red flame shot above the darkened ridge of the mountain, visible to all the awakening towns and villages of the Hudson Valley, dread beacon of another alarming catastrophe in the old resort region of the Catskills. People left their homes in the dawn's growing light and searched the familiar skyline for some identifying landmark. Then peak and clove came full-face into the morning sun and they knew; it was the greatest landmark of all, the Catskill Mountain House, their own expiring glory.*

We have now come four and a quarter miles from the Bastion Falls on Route 23A. I suggest we leave the Escarpment Trail (if we have the time) for a few minutes to go a short distance down the old Mountain House Access Road toward the lakes to another subject of the old souvenir postcards, Alligator Rock. The photos showed this open mouth with upright stones placed so as to make a fairly complete set of teeth. But maybe now the old fellow will need a little help in the way of dental work as "the grinders cease because they are few" and "Remember now thy Creator in the days of thy youth" (Ecclesiastes 12).

Well, now we can backtrack a few hundred years and cross the top of the Otis Incline and skirt past the bathing beach of North Lake Public Campsite. This is the largest public campsite in the Catskills. The North Lake Area totalling some three thousand acres, was purchased around 1930 from the Catskill Mountain House. At that time both lakes were at the same level, which was maintained by a dam at the outlet of South Lake. With the aid of the Civilian Conservation Corps a dam was built at North Lake during the 1930's and the water level in that lake raised.

By subsequent purchases between 1962 and 1967 the State acquired land on South Mountain, the Catskill Mountain House site, South Lake, the Laurel House, Molly Smith's Lookout Point and Rip's Retreat. The total cost of all this land was something less than a million dollars. In connection with the enlargement of the campsite, the State recently removed the North Lake dam and the narrow isthmus between the lakes and built a dam at the outlet of South Lake, making one large lake where for centuries there had been two small ones. Thomas Cole, Asher B. Durand, and other painters of the Hudson River School must be turning over in their graves at this destruction in the name of progress and improvement of one of the mountaintop's most cherished and time-honored motifs.

We move on and leave the lakes behind and travel again along the cliff edge on the top of the Great Wall of Manitou. The next lookout is Artist's Rock, probably named so because Thomas Cole frequently came here, bringing his friends and pointing out to them his house in Catskill, ten miles away. Walking a little farther brings us to Prospect Rock, and still farther and up a little hill is Sunrise Rock where we have an excellent view back to the lake and Mountain House area.

The steep climb of Red Hill brings us to the site of Jacob's Ladder. At one point, many years ago, there was a wooden ladder up the cliff at this point. Unless you are a good rock climber, don't try to scale the ledge here. Turn left and follow the trail around under the ledge and come up on the back side where a yellow marked spur trail will double back to Sunset Rock and a fine view to the south and west. There are several nice lookouts to the east into the Hudson Valley along this spur trail.

Let's go back to the main trail and climb again to Newman's Ledge. This is one of the highest ledges along the way. From here, we look down into the gorge (perhaps "defile" is a better word) where Rip Van Winkle joined the nine-pin bowlers in their refreshment and afterward had his long nap.

It isn't far from here up to a rock shelter known as Badman's Cave. At Badman's Cave, we have come about six miles or a quarter of the way. It is eighteen miles more over North Point, Stopple Point, Arizona, Black Head, Acra Point, Burnt Knob, and Windham High Peak to Route 23. But maybe we should leave that for another day. We can take a yellow cutoff trail from here over to the red trail and return to the North Lake campsite via the red trail and Mary's Glen, or stay on the yellow trail to the campsite gate on the Mountain House Road.

The Escarpment Trail is by no means the easiest trail in the Catskills, but it is surely one of the most rewarding and spectacular, giving back in views and history what it demands in effort. Those who have made that effort will agree that it exemplifies those words, "I love Thy Rocks and Rills, Thy Woods and Templed hills."

Catterskill Falls

Midst greens and shades the Catterskill leaps
From cliffs where the wood-flower clings;
All summer he moistens his verdant steeps
With the sweet light spray of the mountain-
springs,
And he shakes the woods on the mountain-side,
When they drip with the rains of the autumn-tide.

But when, in the forest bare and old,
The blast of December calls,
He builds, in the starlight clear and cold,
A palace of ice where his torrent falls,
With turret, and arch, and fretwork fair,
And pillars blue as the summer air.

William Cullen Bryant

Poet of the Catskills

by Alred H. Marks

The Catskill Mountain House provided the settings for descriptive prose by some of the principal figures of the early 19th century, beginning as early as 1823. Much of that prose has been dutifully collected and republished, first by the Rev. Charles Rockwell[1], and, almost a century later, by Carl Carmer.[2] All of these writings are highly evocative reconstructions of the scene of the Mountain House and journeys to it and about the neighborhood, though some of them sound like testimonials. However much the authors were paid, the result was worth the expense.

The prose statements start with, of all people, Natty Bumpo, James Fenimore Cooper's Leatherstocking, who had a lot to say in *The Pioneers* (1823) about the view from

[1] *The Catskill Mountains and the Region Around*, New York, Taintor Brothers, republished in 1973 by Hope Farm Press, Cornwallville, N. Y.

[2] *The Tavern Lamps Are Burning*, New York: David McKay, 1964.

the front of the hotel and the rest of the scenic wonders roundabout, including Kaaterskill Falls. He probably would have been sent to the service entrance by the doorman if he had tried to enter the hotel's front door, but, then, the old Scout everybody knows was never one for sleeping between sheets and dressing for dinner.

Tyrone Power, the great Irish actor who died in the wreck of the *President* in 1841, also wrote of the view and the Falls, which he visited during his journey about the United States from 1833 to 1835. So did Nathaniel Park Willis, one of the nation's favorite authors from the 1820's to the 1850's. William Cullen Bryant, who ruled the American literary scene with Washington Irving for much of the century, wrote the poem "The Cauterskill Falls" not long before 1887. It is the story of "a youth of dreamy mood" who loses himself in reverie before the falls and has to be resuscitated by passing woodmen.

George William Curtis, editor at different times of *Harper's Weekly* and *Harper's Monthly*, was not entirely taken with the Mountain House or the view. He had evidently traveled too much. He longed for "that true mountain sublimity" one finds in "the presence of lonely snow peaks." He was grateful that he didn't have to come to dinner "in ball costume" and "scramble to the Falls...in varnished pumps." But he was not impressed by the hotel's parlor, which seemed to him to have been struck by a "tempestuous mountain ague." It was "a dangerous parlor for a nervous man." He reported that the hotel promised dancing music in the bar, but "none wished to polk [sic]."

A more permanent visitor and more authoritative literary commentator on the Kaaterskill region, however, was Bliss Carman, who spent almost six months of each year at Twilight Park throughout the first quarter of the twentieth century and wrote many fine poems about what he saw and experienced. Carman is best known, falsely, as poet laureate of Canada, but there is every reason to consider him as not only an important American poet, but also the finest poet of the Catskills.

Carman was a permanent guest of Mary Perry King, who lived with her husband in New Canaan, Connecticut, and spent summers in the impressive cliffside house at Twilight known as Moonshine, from about 1898 until his death in 1929. The poet lived in a small house on the steep incline below the Perry house, which he called "Ghost House" and which he described in great detail in an article in Gustave Stickley's *The Craftsman* magazine in 1906. A great balcony in the living room of the Perry house was the stage for dramatic performances by Mrs. King, Carman and other residents of the colony.

In *The Craftsman* essay, Carman describes the trip up Kaaterskill Clove all the way to his house. His descriptions of the landscape of the area, incidentally, are not obstructed by the forests we know in the late twentieth century:

> *After you have followed this road up the Clove for a mile or two you might look up and see ahead of you on a rounded shoulder of High Peak several houses peeping out of the woods. They are the outposts of Twilight, and you have still a long, steep pull to reach them. At one point not far from here I could put you on a trail that would lead you up through the hemlocks and bring you out almost under the eaves of the Ghost House itself. But unless you are woodwise you would very likely go astray, and anyhow it is a foolish man who puts sign boards along his own trail. So you would have to stick to the road, cheered now and then by glimpses of Ledge*

End Inn and your destination looking down on you, from above, until you turned in at a gate and found yourself at last in Twilight Park.

He published elsewhere a poem that is a companion to that prose statement combining the trip up the Clove and even the mysterious forest shortcut with the view from the other direction, the vantage point of the cabin on the mountainside:

A Mountain Gateway

I know a vale where I would go one day,
When June comes back and all the world once more
Is glad with summer. Deep in shade it lies
A mighty cleft between the bosoming hills,
A cool dim gateway to the mountains' heart.

On either side the wooded slopes come down,
Hemlock and beech and chestnut. Here and there
Through the deep forest laurel spreads and gleams,
Pink-white as Daphne in her loveliness.
Among the sunlit shadows I can see
That still perfection from the world withdrawn,
As if all the wood-gods had arrested there
Immortal beauty in her breathless flight.

The road winds in from the broad river-lands,
Luring the happy traveller turn by turn
Up to the lofty mountains and the sky.
And as he marches with uplifted face,
Far overhead against the arching blue
Gray ledges overhang from dizzy heights,
Scarred by a thousand winters and untamed.

And where the road runs in the valley's foot,
Through the dark woods a mountain stream comes
down,
Singing and dancing all its youth away
Among the boulders and the shallow runs,
Where sunbeams pierce and mossy tree trunks hang
Drenched all day long with murmuring sound and
spray.

There light of heart and footfree, I would go
Up to my home among the lasting hills.
Nearing the day's end, I would leave the road,
Turn to the left and take the steeper trail
That climbs among the hemlocks, and at last
In my own cabin doorway sit me down,
Companioned in that leafy solitude
By the wood ghosts of twilight and of peace,
While evening passes to absolve the day
And leaves the tranquil mountains to the stars.

And in that sweet seclusion I should hear,
Among the cool-leafed beeches in the dusk,
The calm-voiced thrushes at their twilight hymn.
So undistraught, so rapturous, so pure,
They well might be, in wisdom and in joy,
The seraphs singing at the birth of time
The unworn ritual of eternal things.

Carman was a prolific writer of poetry, and some of
his verse is filled with more music than sense, but all his
Catskills poetry is first-rate. He leans heavily on classical
references, as did the nineteenth- century poets that were
his models, but his knowledge of the classics is solid and

seems strengthened by acquaintance with the Greek countryside. Thus his poem in praise of the song of the thrushes
around his cabin is as fine a bird poem as one will find:

Pan in the Catskills

They say that he is dead, and now no more
The reedy syrinx sounds among the hills,
When the long summer heat is on the land.
But I have heard the Catskill thrushes sing,
And therefore am incredulous of death.

In these blue canyons, deep with hemlock shade,
In solitudes of twilight or of dawn,
I have been rapt away from time and care
By the enchantment of a golden strain
As pure as ever pierced the Thracian wild,
Filling the listener with a mute surmise.

At evening and at morning I have gone
Down the cool trail between the beech-tree boles,
And heard the haunting music of the wood
Ring through the silence of the dark ravine,
Flooding the earth with beauty and with joy
And all the ardors of creation old.

And then within my pagan heart awoke
Remembrance of far-off and fabled years
In the untarnished sunrise of the world,
When clear-eyed Hellas in her rapture heard
A slow mysterious piping wild and keen
Thrill through her vales, and whispered, "It is Pan."

Carman seems to have appreciated mornings most in his perch above the Clove. He writes:

If you are like me, your daily routine would be regular, but not inflexible. You would get up early enough to feel the earliness, to taste the freshness and solemnity of the first hours of the day and hear the thrushes at their best. (There are more birds in the woods around the Ghost House than anyone but John Burroughs could name, and nowhere do the thrushes sing more wondrously.)

He expresses elsewhere, in poetry, the joy he gets from mornings in his cabin:

Morning in the Hills

How quiet is the morning in the hills!
The stealthy shadows of the summer clouds
Trail through the canyon, and the mountain
          stream
Sounds his sonorous music far below
In the deep-wooded wind-enchanted cove.

Hemlock and aspen, chestnut, beech, and fir
Go tiering down from storm-worn crest and
          ledge,
While in the hollows of the dark ravine
See the red road emerge, then disappear
Towards the wide plain and fertile valley
          lands.

My forest cabin halfway up the glen
Is solitary, save for one wise thrush,
The sound of falling water, and the wind
Mysteriously conversing with the leaves.

Here I abide unvisited by doubt,
Dreaming of far-off turmoil and despair,
The race of men and love and fleeting time,
What life may be, or beauty, caught and held
For a brief moment at eternal poise.

What impulse now shall quicken and make live
This outward semblance and this inward self?
One breath of being fills the bubble world,
Colored and frail, with fleeting change on change.

Surely some God contrived so fair a thing
In a vast leisure of uncounted days,
And touched it with the breath of living joy,
Wondrous and fair and wise! It must be so.

Only in one poem does Carman come out in his customary poetic pose, as the vagabond, searching the world endlessly for something he once knew in nature to cure the ache in his heart. His poems about the Bay of Fundy area, in a similar mood, earned for him the dubious title of "unofficial Poet Laureate of Canada." This poem, however, is surely about the Catskills:

The Cry of the Hillborn

I am homesick for the mountains—
My heroic mother hills—
And the longing that is on me
No solace ever stills.

I would climb to brooding summits
With their old untarnished dreams,
Cool my heart in forest shadows

Poet

To the lull of falling streams;

Hear the innocence of aspens
That babble in the breeze,
And the fragrant sudden showers
That patter on the trees.

I am lonely for my thrushes
In their hermitage withdrawn,
Toning the quiet transports
Of twilight and of dawn.

I need the pure, strong mornings,
When the soul of day is still,
With the touch of frost that kindles
The scarlet on the hill.

Lone trails and winding woodroads
To outlooks wild and high,
And the pale moon waiting sundown
Where ledges cut the sky.

I dream of upland clearings
Where cones of sumac burn,
And gaunt and gray-mossed boulders
Lie deep in beds of fern;

The gray and mottled beeches,
The birches' satin sheen
The majesty of hemlocks
Crowning the blue ravine.

My eyes dim for the skyline
Where purple peaks aspire,

And the forges of the sunset
Flare up in golden fire.

There crests look down unheeding
And see the great winds blow,
Tossing the huddled tree-tops
In gorges far below;

Where cloud-mists from the warm earth
Roll up about their knees,
And hang their filmy tatters
Like prayers upon the trees.

I cry for night-blue shadows
On plain and hill and dome,—
The spell of old enchantments,
The sorcery of home.

The ghost house is gone now, and one is apt to wonder when looking at the spot where it once stood, how in the world they built it in such a cramped space and how the poet managed to see so much from there. The answers lie, first, as has been said before, in the marvelous forest growth we now enjoy and, second, in the ability of the carpenters of a century ago to build anywhere, given a few feet of footing. We who love the Catskills are fortunate that Bliss Carman managed to secure so firm a foothold in the earth of High Peak ninety years ago.

Rip Van Winkle

Whoever has made a voyage up the Hudson must remember the Kaatskill Mountains. They are a dismembered branch of the great Appalachian family, and are seen away to the West of the river, swelling up to a noble height and lording it over the surrounding country. Every change of season, every change of weather, indeed, every hour of the day, produces some change in the magic hues and shapes of these mountains...When the weather is fair and settled, they are clothed in blue and purple, and print their bold outlines on the clear evening sky; but sometimes, when the rest of the landscape is cloudless, they will gather a hood of gray vapors about their summits, which, in the last rays of the setting sun, will glow and light up like a crown of glory.

Washington Irving

Geology of the Eastern Catskill Escarpment

by Constantine Manos

North Lake and South Lake lie at the eastern edge of the Catskill escarpment, about 1 miles north of Kaaterskill Creek which flows eastward down the very steep incline of the escarpment. The provinces around the lakes and the old Mountain House have long afforded visitors exceptional views of the surrounding countryside. The curious have asked why the land in the Kaaterskill area bears its particular form, with obvious horizontal layering to the bedrock and a soft silhouette to the surrounding heights. To explain these characteristics we need to examine and understand the Catskills themselves.

The Catskill Mountains belong to the physiographic province known as the Appalachian Uplands or the Appalachian Plateaus. But why those mountains? Actually, geologists recognize several types of mountains. They include dome mountains, more or less circular in pattern and marked by a central zone of uplifted rocks, such as the

Adirondacks of New York or the Ozarks of Missouri; and folded mountains which are elongate zones of wrinkled, fractured, and uplifted portions of the earth's crust. The Appalachian Mountains, which trend for more than a thousand miles parallel to the east coast of the United States, are an excellent example of folded mountains. The Catskill Mountains do not fall into either category. Nor are they a highland terrain composed of resistant igneous rocks such as granite, or metamorphic rocks such as gneiss which have been exposed by millions of years of erosion and removal of overlying rock masses. So why those Catskill Mountains?

In physiographic terms the Catskills are definitely a mountain mass. Palenville stands at an elevation of about 540 feet above sea level at the base of the escarpment, some 2,000 feet below the elevation of where the Mountain House stood, two miles to the northwest. This relief, or difference in elevation between mountain crests and adjacent lowlands, is very typical in the Catskills, and while it is not by any means a maximum differential for the Catskills, it certainly indicates true mountainous topography.

The layers of sedimentary rock which make up the Catskills—limestones, shales, siltstones, sandstones and conglomerates—are portions of the earth's crust that have not been severely deformed since they were deposited about 350 to 375 million years ago. Geologists may refer to the Catskills as topographic mountains, underlain by nearly horizontal layers of sedimentary rock. Perhaps more precisely, we can call the Catskill Mountains a dissected plateau, dissected or cut by numerous streams whose network of valleys have established the relief and natural beauty characteristic of the region.

Geology

Rocks of the Catskill Mountains are related o the Appalachian fold belt in a manner not understood by geologists until about 15 years ago when the model of the new global plate tectonics was developed. Our planet has a crust whose thickness ranges from about 6 miles beneath ocean basins to about 25 miles beneath the continents. Below the crust is a zone of the earth called the mantle, which extends to a depth of 1800 miles, where the base of the mantle meets the outer boundary of the earth's core—a compound zone with a radius of about 2150 miles that leads to the center of the earth. Geologists have discovered that the outer part of the earth is broken into nearly two dozen plates, each composed of rocks from the crust and outer part of the mantle, and that these plates have migrated across the earth's surface in various directions relative to each other for much of geologic time. Although the hypothesis of continental drift was introduced many decades ago, the mechanism explaining how the continents could collide, glance past each other in a shearing motion, or separate to form new ocean basins was not fully recognized until recent years.

Most geologists believe the orogenic or mountain-building uplifts of the ancestral Appalachians were caused by crustal plate collisions that progressed and subsided (when the plates changed direction) through many tens of millions of years of geologic time, and that slow-moving but persistent convection currents operating in the earth's mantle have been the driving force for plate motions. The crustal plate carrying early North America collided with plates carrying the developing land masses of Africa and Europe at an elongate collision zone where the rocks of the crust were uplifted, faulted, and folded into a pattern which now shows in the structure of the modern Appalachians. Similar fold structures can be seen in northwest

Africa and in the Caledonian Mountains of northwest Europe. It is interesting to note that if these continents are brought together today, all the Appalachian fold structures produced by the plate collisions show a fairly linear and continuous trend. The continual jigsaw pieces fit, and the patterns of the mountains match.

The first deformation and uplift, or orogeny, of the Appalachian Mountains that affected most of the rocks along its length occurred about 460 million years ago. Sediments carried by streams flowing down the steep mountain slopes were deposited as vast sheets of shales, sandstones, and other rock types along the eastern United States. These sediments, and limestones, were deposited in a vast inland sea that extended from the uplifted mountain range westward toward our present Midwest for hundreds of miles. Although erosion over the next few tens of millions of years reduced the mass and elevation of these mountains to a considerable degree, renewed uplift began during the Devonian Period of geologic time— about 375 million years ago.

This uplift, termed the Acadian Orogeny, was accompanied by the erosion and dispersal of an enormous wedge of sediments from the central parts of the Appalachians in a northwestern direction into the inland or epicontinental sea that lay to the west of the mountains. This wedge of sediments was thickest at the east, near the source terrain where the present sedimentary beds grade into coarse-grained sandstones and conglomerates. The younger rocks nearer the source area are characterized by a red color from relatively small amounts of iron oxide in the sediments. Most of these sediments, and particularly the red beds, were deposited on a vast river or deltaic plain, which probably extended for more than 250 miles, sloping gradually into the epicontinental sea. Farther to the northwest, gray sandstones, siltstones, and shales were deposited in the marine waters. Typical exposures of these Devonian rocks are found in many areas of New York State. The sedimentary rocks are little disturbed today, and mostly show the horizontal or near-horizontal layering developed at the time the sediments were originally deposited.

Since the beginning of the Cenozoic Era about 63 million years ago, the topography of the Appalachians and the Catskill area have been subjected to mild regional uplifts of the crust, and a continuation of the erosion processes which began during the mountain-building phases that formed the Appalachians. Stream downcutting and channel widening in the rocks of the Catskill plateau which were derived by erosion of the Appalachian sourcelands during Devonian time, have developed the landscape we now refer to as the Catskill Mountains.

Within the last one or two million years, vast glaciers advanced to cover about 30 percent of the earth's land surfaces. The continental glaciers which covered virtually all of New York State were about 3,500 feet thick as they passed over and through the Catskill topography. Bedrock surfaces in the Catskills show glacial polish, and striations and grooves scoured into the surfaces by cobbles and boulders that were frozen in the lower surfaces of the ice and dragged along during the glacial movement. Writing for the State University in 1935, John L. Rich reported that some of the ice from the Hudson Valley lobe seems to have spread westward, and even northwestward in parts of the valley of the north fork of Schoharie Creek. Near the Mountain House location there is much evidence of glacial scouring in the bedrock surfaces.

The area around the eastern escarpment shows a coarse textured topography today. The streams are widely separated because the porous rocks such as sandstones tend to absorb much of the runoff from precipitation. It is here that the classic example of steam capture was recognized as the theory itself was developed by N. H. Darton. North and South Lakes, just north of the Mountain House location, were probably the source waters for Gooseberry Creek which flows to the west just below, or south of Tannersville before it joins Schoharie Creek. Waters from the lakes still drain westward for about a mile but are then diverted to the South of Tannersville before it joins Schoharie Creek. Waters from the lakes still drain westward for about a mile but are then diverted to the south at Kaaterskill Creek and flow eastward down a steep gradient past Palenville. Kaaterskill Creek is classified as an obsequent stream because of its steep gradient and direction of flow off the escarpment. It has tended to erode its channel rapidly and lengthen in a headward or upstream direction much faster than streams with only a moderate gradient. The erosion and uphill advance of the Kaaterskill Creek's channel has further captured the headwaters of Gooseberry Creek at Haines Falls, where the Kaaterskill has also intercepted westward flowing waters, diverting them in an eastward direction down the steep slope of the escarpment. The location of the lower Kaaterskill nearer to baselevel, the shorter length of the stream and its gradient, which is so much steeper than the Gooseberry-Schoharie Creek system, have favored the development of this example of stream capture.

In terms of geology, physiography, and stream morphology, the Mountain House area of the Catskill Escarpment is certainly unique. But far from creating just an academic interest, they are the reason for the natural scenic beauty of the Kaaterskill area, a beauty that has evolved over time for all generations to savor.